# THE LITTLE BOOK OF
# SENIOR MOMENTS

THE LITTLE BOOK OF SENIOR MOMENTS

An Hachette UK Company
www.hachette.co.uk

Summersdale Publishers Ltd
Part of Octopus Publishing Group Limited
Carmelite House
50 Victoria Embankment
LONDON
EC4Y 0DZ
UK

www.summersdale.com

Printed and bound in Malta

ISBN: 978-1-84953-789-6

Substantial discounts on bulk quantities of Summersdale books are available to corporations, professional associations and other organisations. For details contact general enquiries: telephone: +44 (0) 1243 771107 or email: enquiries@summersdale.com

# THE LITTLE BOOK OF
# SENIOR
# MOMENTS

## FREDDIE GREEN

TO...............................

FROM...........................

**INSIDE EVERY OLDER PERSON IS A YOUNGER PERSON – WONDERING WHAT THE HELL HAPPENED.**

Cora Harvey Armstrong

**GROWING OLD IS LIKE
BEING INCREASINGLY
PENALISED FOR A CRIME
YOU HAVEN'T COMMITTED.**

Anthony Powell

WHEN YOU DECIDE
AGAINST BUYING
YOUR LITTLE
GRANDSON A JIGSAW
PUZZLE LABELLED
6-8 YEARS. AFTER
ALL, THEY ONLY
HAVE TWO WEEKS
OFF AT CHRISTMAS.

**EVENTUALLY YOU WILL REACH A POINT WHEN YOU STOP LYING ABOUT YOUR AGE AND START BRAGGING ABOUT IT.**

Will Rogers

**EVERY MORNING, LIKE CLOCKWORK, AT 7 A.M., I PEE. UNFORTUNATELY, I DON'T WAKE UP TILL 8.**

Harry Beckworth

WHEN YOU CAN'T
WORK OUT HOW
THE CEREAL GOT
INTO THE FRIDGE,
AND START TO FEEL
NERVOUS ABOUT
WHERE YOU MIGHT
FIND THE MILK.

AS YOU GET OLDER THREE
THINGS HAPPEN. THE FIRST
IS YOUR MEMORY GOES,
AND I CAN'T REMEMBER
THE OTHER TWO...

Norman Wisdom

WHEN YOU
FIND YOURSELF
TOUCHING UP YOUR
CAR'S PAINTWORK
WITH FIXODENT.

WHEN YOU'RE NOT
TOO SURPRISED BY
THE ARRIVAL OF A
NEW FINANCIAL
CRISIS – YOUR
HAIRLINE HAS
ALREADY BEEN
IN RECESSION
FOR 20 YEARS!

**MY DOCTOR TOLD ME
TO DO SOMETHING
THAT PUTS ME OUT OF
BREATH, SO I'VE TAKEN
UP SMOKING AGAIN.**

Jo Brand

# I HAVE THE BODY OF AN 18-YEAR-OLD. I KEEP IT IN THE FRIDGE.

Spike Milligan

WHEN YOU RING
YOUR FRIEND TO
ASK THEM FOR THEIR
PHONE NUMBER.

WHEN YOU INSIST
ON HANDING OUT
NAME BADGES AT ALL
FAMILY GATHERINGS,
ESPECIALLY
SUNDAY LUNCH
WITH YOUR SPOUSE
AND CHILDREN.

**AS FOR ME, EXCEPT FOR AN OCCASIONAL HEART ATTACK, I FEEL AS YOUNG AS I EVER DID.**

Robert Benchley

# I DON'T WANT TO RETIRE. I'M NOT THAT GOOD AT CROSSWORD PUZZLES.

Norman Mailer

**MEN CHASE GOLF BALLS
WHEN THEY'RE TOO OLD
TO CHASE ANYTHING ELSE.**

Groucho Marx

WHEN YOU
FIND YOURSELF
MARVELLING AT
YOUR CAR'S ABILITY
TO MOVE ITSELF
FROM WHERE YOU
PARKED IT.

AS THE TALK TURNS
TO OLD AGE, I SAY I
AM 49 PLUS VAT.

Lionel Blair

I'M OFFICIALLY MIDDLE-AGED. I DON'T NEED DRUGS... I CAN GET THE SAME EFFECT JUST BY STANDING UP REAL FAST.

Jonathan Katz

WHEN YOU ASK
THE GAS MAN TO
WAIT AT THE DOOR
WHILE YOU FETCH
YOUR ORDER FOR
TWO EXTRA SEMI-
SKIMMED AND A
BOTTLE OF ORANGE.

**YOU KNOW YOU ARE GETTING OLDER WHEN 'HAPPY HOUR' IS A NAP.**

Gary Kristofferson

WHEN YOU STOP
ON THE STAIRCASE
TO CATCH YOUR
BREATH, AND CAN'T
REMEMBER WHETHER
YOU WERE GOING
UP OR DOWN.

WHEN YOU ARE
BARRED FROM YOUR
LOCAL SUPERMARKET
FOR CAUSING
CHECKOUT HOLD-UPS
AS YOU TRY TO
REMEMBER YOUR PIN.

**BE KIND TO YOUR KIDS,
THEY'LL BE CHOOSING
YOUR NURSING HOME.**

Anonymous

**INTERVIEWER:** TO WHAT DO YOU ATTRIBUTE YOUR ADVANCED AGE?

**MALCOLM SARGENT:** WELL, I SUPPOSE I MUST ATTRIBUTE IT TO THE FACT THAT I HAVE NOT DIED.

WHEN YOU ANSWER
THE PHONE, ONLY
TO DISCOVER IT
WASN'T YOUR
PHONE THAT WAS
RINGING – IT WAS
ON THE TELEVISION.

WHEN YOU REALISE
THAT'S VASELINE
YOU'RE SPREADING
ON YOUR TOAST,
NOT MARGARINE.

# MY GRANDMOTHER'S 90. SHE'S DATING. HE'S 93. THEY NEVER ARGUE. THEY CAN'T HEAR EACH OTHER.

Cathy Ladman

**FIRST, YOU FORGET NAMES... NEXT, YOU FORGET TO PULL YOUR ZIPPER UP AND FINALLY YOU FORGET TO PULL IT DOWN.**

Leo Rosenberg

**DO NOT WORRY ABOUT
AVOIDING TEMPTATION.
AS YOU GROW OLDER
IT WILL AVOID YOU.**

Anonymous

WHEN YOU FIND THE
PRESENCE OF PUBLIC
TOILET FACILITIES
WORRYINGLY
COMFORTING.

I CAN STILL CUT THE
MUSTARD... I JUST NEED
HELP OPENING THE JAR!

Anonymous

**SEX IN THE SIXTIES IS GREAT, BUT IT IMPROVES IF YOU PULL OVER TO THE SIDE OF THE ROAD.**

Johnny Carson

WHEN YOU ARE OVERWHELMED BY THE URGE TO 'GET HOME, GET SETTLED INTO YOUR TROUSERS WITH THE ELASTICATED WAIST, AND GET THE CURTAINS CLOSED.'

OLD AGE IS LIKE A PLANE
FLYING THROUGH A
STORM. ONCE YOU
ARE ABOARD, THERE IS
NOTHING YOU CAN DO.

Golda Meir

WHEN YOU ARE ANNOYED BY THE FACT THAT YOUR ALL-IN-ONE REMOTE WILL NOT OPEN YOUR GARAGE DOOR. THEN YOU SEE IT'S YOUR MOBILE PHONE.

WHEN YOU
FREQUENTLY
ACQUIRE THIRD-
DEGREE BURNS AT
LUNCH AFTER YOU
ABSENT-MINDEDLY
DIP YOUR HAND
IN YOUR CUP
OF COFFEE FOR
A CHEESE AND
ONION CRISP.

**EXERCISE DAILY. EAT
WISELY. DIE ANYWAY.**

Anonymous

**INTERVIEWER:** CAN YOU REMEMBER ANY OF YOUR PAST LIVES?

**THE DALAI LAMA:** AT MY AGE I HAVE A PROBLEM REMEMBERING WHAT HAPPENED YESTERDAY.

WHEN YOU USE
THE PHRASE 'THE
ONE FROM THE
TV' TO DESCRIBE
WHAT YOU'RE
LOOKING FOR IN
THE SUPERMARKET.

WHEN YOU SPEND
HALF AN HOUR
SEARCHING FOR
YOUR GLASSES, ONLY
TO FIND THAT THEY
WERE ON YOUR HEAD
THE ENTIRE TIME.

**OLD PEOPLE SHOULD NOT EAT HEALTH FOODS. THEY NEED ALL THE PRESERVATIVES THEY CAN GET.**

Robert Orben

**MIDDLE AGE IS WHEN IT TAKES YOU ALL NIGHT TO DO ONCE WHAT ONCE YOU USED TO DO ALL NIGHT.**

Kenny Everett

**I SMOKE 10 TO 15 CIGARS A DAY; AT MY AGE I HAVE TO HOLD ON TO SOMETHING.**

George Burns

WHEN YOU POP OUT
FOR MILK AND COME
HOME WITH A NEW
DOG COLLAR, RAWL
PLUGS, SOME PLANT
POTS THAT WERE ON
SPECIAL OFFER...
BUT NO MILK.

# WHEN WE'RE YOUNG WE WANT TO CHANGE THE WORLD. WHEN WE'RE OLD WE WANT TO CHANGE THE YOUNG.

Anonymous

# DON'T LET AGEING GET YOU DOWN. IT'S TOO HARD TO GET BACK UP.

John Wagner

WHEN YOU DECIDE
IT'S TIME TO PULL
UP YOUR SOCKS,
AND REALISE
YOU FORGOT TO
PUT ANY ON.

**LONG AFTER WEARING BIFOCALS AND HEARING AIDS, WE'LL STILL BE MAKING LOVE. WE JUST WON'T KNOW WITH WHOM.**

Jack Paar

WHEN YOU REMARK
THAT YOU HAVEN'T
SEEN THE QUEEN
MOTHER ON THE
TV FOR A WHILE.

WHEN YOU
SUDDENLY WONDER
WHY THERE ARE SO
MANY CARS DRIVING
ON THE WRONG SIDE
OF THE ROAD TODAY.

**EARLY TO RISE AND EARLY TO BED MAKES A MAN HEALTHY, WEALTHY AND DEAD.**

James Thurber

MIDDLE AGE IS WHEN YOUR OLD CLASSMATES ARE SO GREY AND WRINKLED AND BALD THEY DON'T RECOGNISE YOU.

Bennett Cerf

WHEN YOU TELEPHONE A RELATIVE FROM ABROAD FOR THEIR FULL ADDRESS, SO YOU CAN SEND A POSTCARD AND LET THEM KNOW HOW YOU'RE GETTING ON.

WHEN YOU MENTION
TO A FRIEND THAT
YOU MUST PHONE
THEM WHEN YOU
GET THE CHANCE.

**GRANT ME CHASTITY
AND CONTINENCE,
BUT NOT YET.**

Augustine of Hippo

# THE OLDER WE GET, THE BETTER WE USED TO BE.

John McEnroe

A MAN LOSES HIS
ILLUSIONS FIRST, HIS
TEETH SECOND AND
FOLLIES LAST.

Helen Rowland

WHEN YOU BECOME
FRUSTRATED BY
INSTRUCTIONS TO
'PRESS ANY KEY' –
WHY WOULD THEY
TELL YOU TO DO
THAT WHEN THERE'S
NO 'ANY' KEY ON
YOUR KEYBOARD?

**YOU KNOW YOU'RE
GETTING OLD WHEN
YOUR IDEA OF A HOT,
FLAMING DESIRE IS A
BARBECUED STEAK.**

Victoria Fabiano

# MIDDLE AGE IS WHEN YOUR AGE STARTS TO SHOW AROUND YOUR MIDDLE.

Bob Hope

WHEN YOU TAKE
THE BUS INTO TOWN
AND END UP IN THE
NEXT COUNTY,
WITH ONLY A VAGUE
RECOLLECTION OF A
DREAM INVOLVING
TOASTED TEACAKES.

# DO I EXERCISE? WELL, I ONCE JOGGED TO THE ASHTRAY.

Will Self

WHEN YOUR
EFFORTS TO CATCH
THE ATTENTION OF A
FRIEND IN THE STREET
ARE MET WITH LOOKS
OF TERROR AS YOU
DRAW NEARER
AND EMBRACE
A COMPLETE
STRANGER.

WHEN THE STRAINED
LOOKS ON THE
FACES OF YOUR
FRIENDS AND FAMILY
TELL YOU THEY
HAVE HEARD THIS
STORY BEFORE.
MANY TIMES.

**MY NAN SAID, 'WHAT DO YOU MEAN WHEN YOU SAY THE COMPUTER WENT DOWN ON YOU?'**

Joe Longthorne

YOUTH IS WHEN YOU'RE
ALLOWED TO STAY UP
LATE ON NEW YEAR'S EVE;
MIDDLE AGE IS WHEN
YOU'RE FORCED TO.

William E. Vaughn

WHEN YOU MISTAKE
YOUR ELECTRIC
BLANKET KICKING IN
FOR A HOT FLUSH.

WHEN THE LOCAL
CHARITY SHOP
IS VERY PLEASED
TO ACCEPT YOUR
DONATION OF
BRAND-NEW
CLOTHES, STILL
IN THEIR BAGS
FROM YESTERDAY'S
SHOPPING TRIP.

**ALWAYS PAT CHILDREN ON THE HEAD WHENEVER YOU MEET THEM, JUST IN CASE THEY HAPPEN TO BE YOURS.**

Augustus John

## IN DOG YEARS, I'M DEAD.

Anonymous

**TRUE TERROR IS TO WAKE
UP ONE MORNING AND
DISCOVER THAT YOUR
HIGH SCHOOL CLASS IS
RUNNING THE COUNTRY.**

Kurt Vonnegut

WHEN YOU SEARCH
HIGH AND LOW
IN THE PANTRY
CUPBOARD AND
STILL CAN'T
FIND YOUR OLD
SPICE POWDER.

# MIDDLE AGE IS HAVING A CHOICE BETWEEN TWO TEMPTATIONS AND CHOOSING THE ONE THAT'LL GET YOU HOME EARLIER.

Dan Bennett

# I REFUSE TO ADMIT THAT I AM MORE THAN 52, EVEN IF THAT MAKES MY CHILDREN ILLEGITIMATE.

Nancy Astor

WHEN YOUR 'GREEN
WASTE' RECYCLING
BIN CONTAINS ITEMS
SUCH AS GREEN TEA
BAGS, SALT AND
VINEGAR CRISP
PACKETS, AND THOSE
LIME-FLAVOURED
FRUIT GUMS YOU'RE
NOT SO KEEN ON.

WHEN YOUR DENTIST
SEEMS A BIT BAFFLED
AS YOU START TO
UNDRESS FOR YOUR
YEARLY CHECK-UP.

# ANYONE CAN GET OLD. ALL YOU HAVE TO DO IS LIVE LONG ENOUGH.

Groucho Marx

**THERE WILL ALWAYS
BE DEATH AND TAXES;
HOWEVER, DEATH DOESN'T
GET WORSE EVERY YEAR.**

Anonymous

WHEN YOU
FIND YOURSELF
WONDERING HOW
IT'S POSSIBLE TO
HAVE A HUNDRED
CHANNELS ON YOUR
TV BUT NOTHING
WORTH WATCHING
ON ANY OF THEM.

WHEN A NEIGHBOUR
REMARKS UPON
HOW WELL YOUR
RUBBER GLOVES
COMPLEMENT YOUR
EVENING DRESS.

# I KNOW I CAN'T CHEAT DEATH, BUT I CAN CHEAT OLD AGE.

Darwin Deason

# I DON'T HAVE ANY CHILDREN, I HAVE FOUR MIDDLE-AGED PEOPLE.

Dick Van Dyke

WHEN YOU REQUEST
A RING AND RIDE
PICK-UP FROM
YOUR ADDRESS OF
30 YEARS PAST.

WHEN YOU KINDLY
OFFER A GUEST
FREE CHOICE FROM
YOUR BOWL OF
ORNAMENTAL FRUIT.

# I CAN STILL ENJOY SEX AT 74. I LIVE AT 75, SO IT'S NO DISTANCE.

Bob Monkhouse

THE YEARS BETWEEN 50
AND 70 ARE THE HARDEST.
YOU ARE ALWAYS
ASKED TO DO THINGS,
AND YET YOU ARE NOT
DECREPIT ENOUGH TO
TURN THEM DOWN.

T. S. Eliot

# YOUTH IS THE TIME OF GETTING, MIDDLE AGE OF IMPROVING AND OLD AGE OF SPENDING.

Anne Bradstreet

WHEN YOU REQUIRE
A PEN AND PAPER
TO ORDER A ROUND
OF DRINKS.

OLD AGE HAS ITS
PLEASURES, WHICH,
THOUGH DIFFERENT,
ARE NOT LESS THAN THE
PLEASURES OF YOUTH.

W. Somerset Maugham

**MEMORIAL SERVICES ARE THE COCKTAIL PARTIES OF THE GERIATRIC SET.**

Harold Macmillan

WHEN YOU THINK
MR BEAN ISN'T
HALF AS FUNNY
AS HE USED TO BE,
AND THEN REALISE
YOU'RE WATCHING
A POLITICAL PARTY
CONFERENCE
SPEECH.

YOU KNOW YOU'RE
GETTING OLD WHEN THE
CANDLES COST MORE
THAN THE CAKE.

Bob Hope

WHEN, AFTER BRUSHING SEVERAL TIMES WITH DISAPPOINTING RESULTS, YOU READ THE FINE PRINT AND DISCOVER THAT ANUSOL IS NOT, IN FACT, A BRAND OF TOOTHPASTE.

WHEN YOU FIND
YOURSELF ENJOYING
A HEALTHY
MORNING BOWL
OF KITTY BITES.

**THE PAST IS THE ONLY DEAD THING THAT SMELLS SWEET.**

Cyril Connolly

WHEN YOU
FIND YOURSELF
WONDERING IF
THERE'S ANYTHING
THAT MOBILE
PHONES *CAN'T*
DO NOWADAYS.

## THE FIRST 100 YEARS
## ARE THE HARDEST.

Wilson Mizner

# THE FIRST SIGN OF MATURITY IS THE DISCOVERY THAT THE VOLUME KNOB ALSO TURNS TO THE LEFT.

Jerry M. Wright

**THE THREE AGES OF MAN: YOUTH, MIDDLE AGE AND 'MY WORD YOU DO LOOK WELL'.**

June Whitfield

WHEN YOU CALL
YOUR PARTNER BY
YOUR PET'S NAME,
AND VICE VERSA.

**NICE TO BE HERE? AT MY AGE IT'S NICE TO BE ANYWHERE.**

George Burns

I DON'T FEEL OLD. I
DON'T FEEL ANYTHING
TILL NOON. THAT'S WHEN
IT'S TIME FOR MY NAP.

Bob Hope

WHEN YOU
EVENTUALLY
MANAGE TO MAKE
IT TO THE TOP OF
THE LADDER BEFORE
IT DAWNS ON YOU
THAT IT'S AGAINST
THE WRONG WALL.

**I USED TO THINK I'D LIKE LESS GREY HAIR. NOW I'D LIKE MORE OF IT.**

Richie Benaud

WHEN YOUR FRIEND
ARRIVES AT THE
ALLOTMENT, AND
ASKS HOW LONG
IT HAS TAKEN YOU
TO WEED AND
HOE HIS PATCH.

WHEN YOU REACH
FOR YOUR 5-IRON,
AND PULL OUT YOUR
NEW, LIGHTWEIGHT
WALKING STICK.

## AT MY AGE 'GETTING LUCKY' MEANS FINDING MY CAR IN THE PARKING LOT.

Anonymous

**THE EASIEST WAY TO DIMINISH THE APPEARANCE OF WRINKLES IS TO KEEP YOUR GLASSES OFF WHEN YOU LOOK IN THE MIRROR.**

Joan Rivers

WHEN ALL YOUR
INTERACTIONS WITH
YOUNG PEOPLE
BEGIN, 'AH, BUT
BACK IN *MY* DAY...'

**WHEN EVERY PARTY IS NOW A SURPRISE PARTY – INCLUDING THE ONES YOU HOST.**

**AS WE GROW OLDER, OUR BODIES GET SHORTER AND OUR ANECDOTES LONGER.**

Robert Quillen

**EVERYTHING SLOWS DOWN WITH AGE, EXCEPT THE TIME IT TAKES CAKE AND ICE CREAM TO REACH YOUR HIPS.**

John Wagner

**YOU'RE GETTING OLD
WHEN THE ONLY THING
YOU WANT FOR YOUR
BIRTHDAY IS NOT TO
BE REMINDED OF IT.**

Anonymous

WHEN YOU WONDER
IF YOU CAN TRAVEL
THROUGH THE EU
ON YOUR BUS PASS.

**EACH YEAR IT GROWS HARDER TO MAKE ENDS MEET – THE ENDS I REFER TO ARE HANDS AND FEET.**

Richard Armour

IF YOU RESOLVE TO GIVE UP SMOKING, DRINKING AND LOVING, YOU DON'T ACTUALLY LIVE LONGER. IT JUST SEEMS LONGER.

Clement Freud

WHEN SOMEONE
ASKS YOU HOW
LARGE YOUR CARBON
FOOTPRINT IS, AND
YOU REPLY, 'I'M SO
SORRY, I THOUGHT
I WIPED MY FEET
AS I CAME IN!'

I BELIEVE IN LOYALTY.
WHEN A WOMAN REACHES
A CERTAIN AGE SHE
LIKES, SHE SHOULD
STICK WITH IT.

Eva Gabor

WHEN YOU SPEND THE
AFTERNOON GOING
THROUGH OLD PHOTO
ALBUMS, BUT CAN'T
REMEMBER WHO ANY
OF THE PEOPLE ARE
IN THE PICTURES.

WHEN NO MATTER
HOW MUCH YOU
ADJUST YOUR
TURNTABLE, IT
SIMPLY WILL NOT
PLAY YOUR NEW
MICHAEL BUBLÉ CD.

**OLD AGE AND TREACHERY
WILL ALWAYS BEAT YOUTH
AND EXUBERANCE.**

David Mamet

**FUN IS LIKE LIFE INSURANCE; THE OLDER YOU GET, THE MORE IT COSTS.**

Kin Hubbard

WHEN AFTER
QUEUING FOR HALF
AN HOUR TO BUY
STAMPS IN THE
POST OFFICE, YOU
FORGET TO STICK
THEM ON ANY OF
YOUR LETTERS.

WHEN YOU ARE
THOROUGHLY
DISAPPOINTED TO
DISCOVER THAT A
NEW LOCAL SHOP
'YOUR S&M' IS
NOT A MARKS AND
SPENCER'S OUTLET.

**YOU CAN JUDGE YOUR AGE BY THE AMOUNT OF PAIN YOU FEEL WHEN YOU COME IN CONTACT WITH A NEW IDEA.**

Pearl S. Buck

**I DON'T NEED YOU TO REMIND ME OF MY AGE. I HAVE A BLADDER TO DO THAT FOR ME.**

Stephen Fry

**WISDOM DOESN'T
NECESSARILY COME WITH
AGE. SOMETIMES AGE JUST
SHOWS UP ALL BY ITSELF.**

Tom Wilson

WHEN YOU
AUTOMATICALLY
CONVERT
EVERY METRIC
MEASUREMENT INTO
'OLD MONEY' IN
ORDER TO WORK
OUT HOW BIG
IT REALLY IS.

# FOR ALL THE ADVANCES IN MEDICINE, THERE IS STILL NO CURE FOR THE COMMON BIRTHDAY.

John Glenn

# YOUTH IS A WONDERFUL THING. WHAT A CRIME TO WASTE IT ON CHILDREN.

George Bernard Shaw

WHEN THE PETROL
STATION ATTENDANT
TELLS YOU HOW
MUCH YOUR FUEL
COMES TO, AND
YOU THINK THEY
MUST BE SELLING
YOU ANOTHER CAR.

I PLAN ON GROWING OLD
MUCH LATER IN LIFE, OR
MAYBE NOT AT ALL.

Patty Carey

**WHEN THE CROCHETED BOBBLE HAT YOU'RE WEARING LOOKS REMARKABLY LIKE YOUR TEA COSY.**

WHEN TODAY'S NEWSPAPER SEEMS STRANGELY FAMILIAR – THEY'VE EVEN REPEATED YESTERDAY'S FRONT PAGE HEADLINE!

I AM GETTING TO AN AGE
WHEN I CAN ONLY ENJOY
THE LAST SPORT LEFT. IT
IS CALLED HUNTING FOR
YOUR SPECTACLES.

Edward Grey

**THE ELDERLY DON'T DRIVE
THAT BADLY; THEY'RE JUST
THE ONLY ONES WITH TIME
TO DO THE SPEED LIMIT.**

Jason Love

WHEN YOU STOP TO
ADMIRE THE SNOWY
HILLS IN VIEW OF
YOUR HOUSE AND
DISCOVER (AFTER
FIVE YEARS OF
LIVING THERE)
THAT THEY ARE
CHALK CLIFFS.

WHEN YOU WONDER
WHY YOUR COAT
APPEARS TO HAVE A
KINK IN IT, ON SEEING
YOUR REFLECTION
IN A SHOP WINDOW,
AND LATER FIND THAT
THE COAT HANGER
IS STILL INSIDE.

**I DON'T DO ALCOHOL ANY MORE – I GET THE SAME EFFECT JUST STANDING UP FAST.**

Anonymous

**WHENEVER A MAN'S FRIENDS BEGIN TO COMPLIMENT HIM ABOUT LOOKING YOUNG, HE MAY BE SURE THAT THEY THINK HE IS GROWING OLD.**

Washington Irving

# MIDDLE AGE IS WHEN YOUR BROAD MIND AND NARROW WAIST BEGIN TO CHANGE PLACES.

E. Joseph Cossman

WHEN YOU RESORT
TO OPENING A
CHILDPROOF LID
WITH A MALLET.

**OLD PEOPLE ARE FOND OF
GIVING GOOD ADVICE;
IT CONSOLES THEM
FOR NO LONGER BEING
CAPABLE OF SETTING
A BAD EXAMPLE.**

François de La Rochefoucauld

# YOU KNOW YOU'RE OLD IF THEY HAVE DISCONTINUED YOUR BLOOD TYPE.

Phyllis Diller

WHEN YOU CALL YOUR PHONE COMPANY TO COMPLAIN THAT YOUR NEW, HIGH-SPEED BROADBAND BOX CAN'T EVEN GET RADIO 4.

**TO ME, OLD AGE IS ALWAYS 15 YEARS OLDER THAN I AM.**

Bernard Baruch

WHEN YOU FIND
VEGETABLE
PEELINGS IN THE
CLOTHES BASKET,
AND SUDDENLY
UNDERSTAND WHY
THE WASTE DISPOSAL
UNIT IS BLOCKED.

# THE SECRET TO STAYING YOUNG IS TO LIVE HONESTLY, EAT SLOWLY AND LIE ABOUT YOUR AGE.

Lucille Ball

YOU CAN LIVE TO BE 100
IF YOU GIVE UP ALL THE
THINGS THAT MAKE YOU
WANT TO LIVE TO BE 100.

Woody Allen

**BIRTHDAYS ARE GOOD
FOR YOU. STATISTICS
SHOW THAT THE PEOPLE
WHO HAVE THE MOST
LIVE THE LONGEST.**

Larry Lorenzoni

WHEN YOU GO
UPSTAIRS TO GET
SOMETHING, FORGET
WHAT IT WAS, AND
COME DOWNSTAIRS
WITH SOMETHING
ELSE YOU DIDN'T
KNOW YOU NEEDED.

SURE I'M FOR HELPING THE
ELDERLY. I'M GOING TO BE
OLD MYSELF SOMEDAY.

Lillian Gordy Carter

**AGE IS AN ISSUE OF
MIND OVER MATTER.
IF YOU DON'T MIND,
IT DOESN'T MATTER.**

Mark Twain

If you're interested in finding
out more about our books,
find us on Facebook at
**SUMMERSDALE PUBLISHERS**
and follow us on Twitter at
**@SUMMERSDALE.**


**WWW.SUMMERSDALE.COM**